ALBERTO PINTO
Classics

ALBERTO PINTO
Classics

RIZZOLI
NEW YORK

First published in the United States of America in 2001 by
Rizzoli International Publications, Inc.
3oo Park Avenue South, New York, NY 10010

ISBN: 0-8478-2411-X
LCCN: 2001087580

Designed by Alain Pouyer

Cover: sitting room in Alberto Pinto's apartment *On the Quai d'Orsay* (pp.248-249)
Page two: Carrier-belleuse statue in the Hersant Mansion *On the Champ de Mars* (pp.22-23)
Page eight: detail of living room from *For an art collector* (pp.70-71)
Page ten: sitting room *A ranch in the desert* (p.158)
Back cover: entrance hall of Hersant Mansion with replica of eighteenth-century marble group
by Lemoine from *On the Champ de Mars* (p.13)

Distributed by St. Martin's Press

Printed and bound in Singapore

CONTENTS

We would like to thank the following people
for their assistance:

Nicole Fallot, project coordinator;
Bruno Roy for floral arrangements and
styling; Marianne Robic; Flowers by
ZeZe NY, floral decorations.

Sincere thanks also go to the entire staff
of Alberto Pinto's design studio for their
sound advice.

P.R.
W.W.

ALBERTO PINTO belongs to that closed circle of highly talented interior decorators known throughout the world. Before becoming a full-fledged decorator in the seventies, he developed a critical eye as director of a photography agency specializing in architecture and interior design. Working with the Condé Nast Group, Maison Française, Elle and other magazines gave him the opportunity to clarify his ideas on design in Italy, work on spatial and chromatic organization with Luis Barragan in Mexico and admire the unique savvy of David Hicks. Since then, Alberto Pinto and his design studio, currently located in Paris near the Place des Victoires, have earned their stripes as past masters in the fine art of creating custom houses where elegance and abundance are in harmonious balance. Few people have such unfailing intuition about furniture and *objets d'art*.

Alberto Pinto's roots are Moroccan; from his land, he has kept a generous, easy-going smile that gives substance to seemingly unimportant everyday details. His childhood memories are not at all remarkable: he remembers himself as calm, well-behaved and happy in an open, uncomplicated family. Paris exerted a great influence on taste in post-colonial Casablanca, his hometown,and quite unsurprisingly, the young Alberto preferred faraway French influences to nearby Moroccan ones. However, once mastered and understood, his instincts would fashion his unique savoir-faire. As time passed, he realized that his attraction to daring juxtaposition, his lavish use of color and love of comfort, as well as his sense of pomp, were derivative of Oriental traditions. From his travels, he amassed the quintessence of worlds of design— French elegance, British chic and American rationalism among them. His style easily appeals to an international clientele whose occupations and tastes tend by their very nature to the eclectic.

Raised in a large home, Alberto Pinto has always remained attached to wide open spaces—indoors—almost gigantic in proportion. From his youth in Casablanca, he remembers family traditions that involved the constant comings and goings of numerous friends; there was always room for one more at the dinner table. Entertaining was an intuitive art based on centuries of Oriental customs. For Alberto, narrow-minded egocentricity need not be the price paid for calm and tranquillity.

His approach tends to enlarge available space: a pushing-back-the-walls philosophy associated with an intuitive avoidance of banal box structures. When he creates intimate areas in more limited confines, nothing is obvious. Bedrooms take on the comfortable airs of drawing rooms; drawing rooms forget to be grandiloquent and become cozy spots ideal for restful evenings with close friends.

Pinto would prefer to be considered as an *éminence grise* in the grand tradition, beguiling but discreet, ever in the shadow

of the Great, shaping their lifestyles, and, to a certain extent, their image. He would say that he simply makes himself available to his clients as the organizer of their daily life. *L'homme pressé*, the legendary character invented by Paul Morand, is the implicit model. And as chance would have it, Alberto Pinto resided in the author's Paris apartment overlooking the Champ de Mars.

Color and warmth are avowed necessities: memories of the Moroccan climate were most certainly a decisive factor here.Cold and uninviting interiors are thus banished from his repertoire. Choices are intended to reassure. Instead of launching new styles that challenge existing canons of taste— an exercise that does not appeal to him—Pinto practices in his own subtle manner another form of provocation. Ancient memories surge forth as he deftly manipulates classic styles with a twist. Geographical context and the corresponding ambience are more often mixed than matched. Refusing to turn his back on his roots, Pinto fancies best the Orient in European and especially French interiors. Slightly discordant crosscurrents add unexpected freshness. Pinto's penchant for Russian furnishings, especially those of his much-beloved 19th century, has lead him often to recreate delightfully nostalgic decors.

When the style is Spanish-American, he delves into childhood memories linked to Hollywood movies, especially westerns where Indians and cowboys rarely see eye to eye. In Paris, Alberto Pinto often receives commissions for the renovation of private mansions playing a part in the history of the capital.

A cultivated but decidedly eclectic approach to design is probably Pinto's strong point. This brings him in regular contact with highly skilled craftsmen and gifted artists. It is worth mentioning that Alberto Pinto is one of the few important interior decorators who is constantly discovering new talent among young craftsmen. He knows that without them his ideas could not take shape.

On the Champ de Mars in Paris

A fervent art collector, the first owner of the mansion received a replica from the Louvre Museum of the 18th-century marble group by Jean-François Lemoine in thanks for his gift of the original to the art institution. Placed in the entrance hall, this precious object prepares visitors for the many art treasures reigning in this neoclassical French mansion.

More than nine hundred blue and white Chinese porcelain pieces line the walls of the entrance hall, presented symmetrically on baroque giltwood consoles from an Italian palace.

On the prestigious Champ de Mars in Paris, at the foot of the Eiffel Tower, stands the Hersant mansion. At the turn of the 20th century, this was the magnificent home of a powerful French industrialist who dug the Tonkin Canal and was instrumental in the modernization of Morocco. The work of the architect Sergent, who also designed the Camondo mansion near the Parc Monceau, the mansion is of classical French inspiration. In the twenties and thirties, frequent parties here brought together the cream of Paris society, so much so that a large addition was built on the garden side. Alberto Pinto was commissioned by an international businessman to transform the mansion into a veritable summer palace, more adapted to important business conferences than society receptions. In order to realize the owner's wishes and create an air of stately grandeur, Pinto respected the initial floor plan; he did, however, change some flooring and embellish certain rooms with antique wood boiseries.

*Reminiscent of German Rococo
decoration in Charlottenburg Palace,
the walls of the entrance hall are
literally covered with a unique collection
of 17th-century Chinese porcelain
presented on ornate wooden consoles.
Nearly all of the pieces come from a
Dutch vessel shipwrecked in 1680.
The cargo was recovered three hundred
years later and acquired by the present
owner at an auction at Christie's.*

*Above: A staircase off the central
rotonda. Opposite: In the center of the
inlaid marble floor stands an Italian
table and a 1930 cloisonné vase. The
oval-shaped landscapes with classical
ruins are by 18th-century French
painter Hubert Robert.*

The state dining room is lined with mahogany and gold leaf wooden paneling. Louis XIV-style furnishings evoke quintessential French elegance.

French table art first pleases the eye and then the palate. Alberto Pinto is at his best when he stages elegant dining rooms. He knows how to achieve the delicate balance between comfort and refinement, how antique wood paneling creates warm intimacy, and which lighting will make crystal, silver and porcelain best sparkle. The antique dark mahogany and gold leaf boiseries are French. The panels are lined with 18th-century porcelain. Giltwood chandeliers in the Louis XIV-style illuminate the floral patterns on the ceiling, inspired by Vincennes porcelain designs. Crimson velvet and giltwood chairs also evoke the *Roi Soleil*.

A vermeil plate with the Rothschild's coat of arms rests on embroidered linen. The glasses are 19th-century cut crystal.

The Louis XIV-style smoking room is a harbor of tranquillity, steeped in the harmonies of dark wood, royal blue and gold. The dark oak paneling is decorated with stencilled Regency designs. Regency and Louis XIV giltwood furniture surround a blue silk velvet sofa set on a Savonnerie rug. The large looking glass was executed by Baccarat crystalworks in the 19th century for a palace on the Bosporus. The chandelier is in Italian rock crystal.

The Louis XIV sitting room precedes the main salon. The classical French floor plan has been respected with its long succession of reception halls. Light floods in these garden-side rooms through tall windows. Tones of pale blue set off the large paintings by Hubert Robert which had formerly hung in the smoking room. The light-colored Louis XIV paneling enhanced with simple gold designs is the perfect backdrop for the dramatic landscapes. The Louis XIV medallion armchairs and other sitting furniture carry the stamp of Boulard, the cabinetmaker. A Carrier-Belleuze terracotta statue sits atop a hardstone gueridon by Thomire, the foremost bronze craftsman in the Neoclassical style. Pinto redesigned the ceiling in the Neo-Pompeian style so dear to Marie Antoinette. The delicate Russian crystal chandelier came from the Kugel antique dealers in Paris. The floor is covered with an immense Savonnerie rug.

Situated between the Louis XIV smoking room and the "salon bleu" in the Regency style, the Louis XVI sitting room provides a light touch in the pomp of this grandiloquent interior.

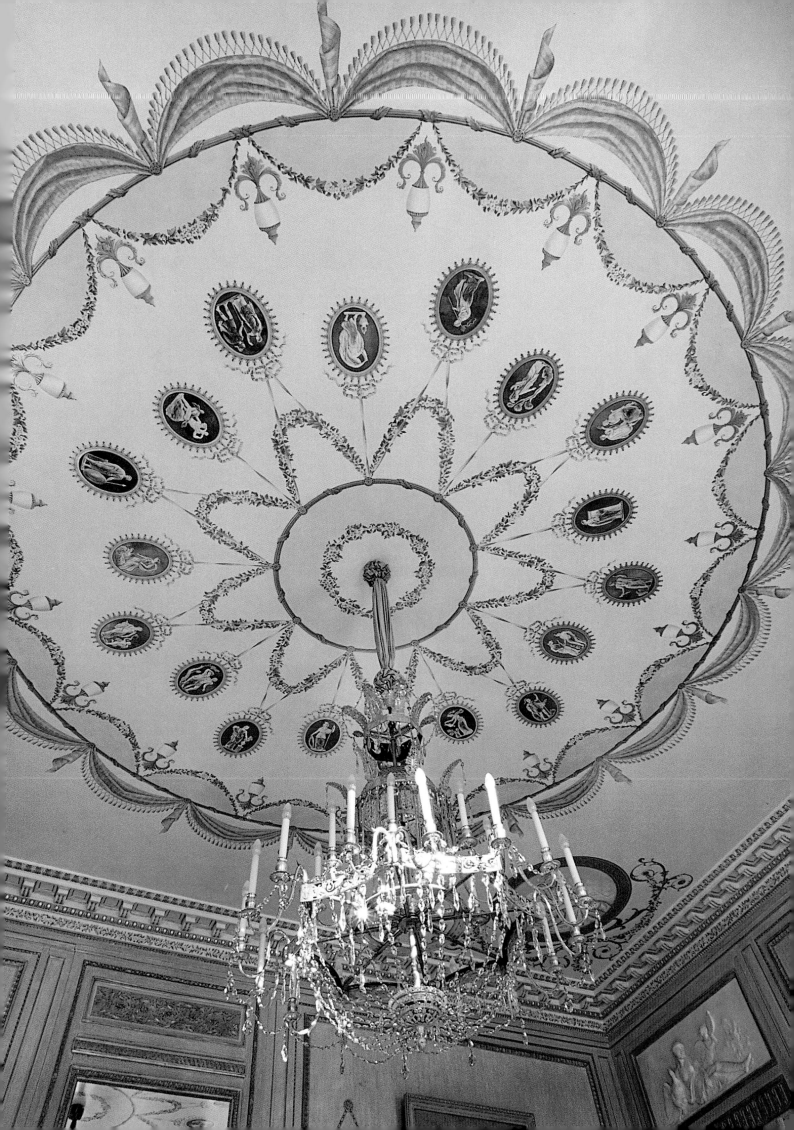

View of two of the reception rooms. Sèvres porcelain jardinières flank a marble chimney mantle. Next to it, one of a pair of black Chinese lacquer commodes in the style of the cabinetmaker Carlin. Alabaster vases complete the Neoclassical theme of the salon.

The *salon bleu* is the epitome of stately interior design in the French style. The private apartments of Madame de Pompadour and her brother, Marquis de Marigny, in the Elysée Palace – the current residence of the presidents of the French republic – are brought to mind. Enhanced by simple gold designs, the dark carved-wood paneling adds strict symmetry and princely splendor as do the Boulle *bibliothèques* flanking the fireplace. Under the floor-to-ceiling mirror, Pinto creates a more intimate seating arrangement for quiet conversation. The cold, bluish light in the winter scene by Monet harmonizes with the blue shades of Sèvres and Chinese porcelain which Pinto chose for the salon. The Regency seating furniture once graced the Rothschild mansion on Avenue Foch in Paris—and the chinoiserie carpet, the Château des Mirandes, Josephine Baker's retreat.

Reminiscent of the popular 18th-century theme of frolicking monkeys imitating humans, the carved wood paneling, decorated with allegorical scenes, creates a baroque feeling in the master study.

The walls of the master study are lined with remarkable carved wood paneling. The sculpted motifs are in gold leaf against a light background. Dresden porcelain objects are grouped in display cases and on consoles: monkeys musicians and Italian figures mingle in this Rococo-style decor. A classical French bureau with sensuous Baroque lines has been placed near the marble fireplace. Louis XVI armchairs and a Regency leather chair are nearby. A Savonnerie rug in the Neoclassical style covers the parquet floor.

The master bedroom was formerly a
study. The dark boiserie provided the
perfect backdrop for Boulle furniture
from the Patino collection and paintings
by Matisse and Renoir.

Detail of the the silk brocade draperies.

A carved giltwood looking glass flanked
by small lamps reflects a hardstone urn
lamp and a portrait by Renoir.

With all doors closed, the master dressing room becomes an elegant antichamber.

The austere lines of the master bath harmonize with the original stucco walls. The intricate patterns of the marble marquetry floor are borrowed from Italian cathedral paving. Pinto disguises the functionality of this bathroom, which more resembles a comfortable sitting room. The sink is encased in a marquetry cabinet and the tub is transformed into a marble fountain.

Alberto Pinto knows that true luxury is judged by those parts of an interior only accessible to those who live in it. This dressing room is an excellent case in point. The decorator excels in creating elegant functionality for men's clothes: generous closet space is allotted for suits and jackets, special tie racks, shoe stands and wide shelves for shirts and sweaters. Doors and walls are decorated with panels of Empire-style wood marquetry. Opened wide, the closets proudly display the wide range of apparel. When closed, the room becomes an elegant antechamber.

The master bath with the original stucco walls.

Sèvres porcelain flowers compete with perfumed roses from the garden against a background of embroidered silk and Calais lace.

The bedroom of the lady of the house is quite naturally decorated with feminine, embroidered fabrics in intricate pleats and drapery. Fans have been chosen as the leitmotif. A collection of antique models is presented on an English mahogany folding screen (pages 40–41) and hung on the walls (opposite). Watercolors of fans hide closets behind them. The canopy bed is English Georgian. Floral print silk is used for the window draperies and the bed canopy, while embroidered silk covered with Calais lace graces the walls. The Anglo-Chinese theme is enhanced by Louis XVI furniture and a pair of small cabriolet armchairs with precious Chinese lacquer backs from the 1920s. The Empire armchairs with eagle-head armrests are Russian and were once part of the Pavlosk Palace collection.

This rare matching pair of armchairs from Pavlosk Palace is covered with painted, embroidered silk featuring festoons of flowers. Their imposing imperial design is metamorphosed into elegant coquetry.

The lady's bathroom with
trompe l'œil murals
becomes an italian grotto.

The lady's bathroom is delightfully whimsical. Pinto employed trompe l'œil murals presenting wooded landscape to soften rather massive architectural details. A heavy vault becomes a cool Italian grotto. Crystal chandeliers add elegant frivolousness.

Following pages: The summer dining room brings to mind the carefree and elegant atmosphere of certain hotels in Brighton, England. Walls are covered with a chinoiserie wallpaper and the tent ceiling also contributes to the pleasure pavilion theme. The crystal chandeliers are curiously shaped globes that once hung in the casino in Deauville. The three round tables can be joined together for more formal dining by adding extra leaves.

An apartment in Paris

In the foyer, guests are greeted by a bronze bust of Molière placed against wood paneling with stencilled gold leaf motifs, a hint of the theatrical stages to follow. In the sitting room, the severity of the Regency boiserie, with carved wood and gold panels, is softened by scarlet velvet sofas and bergère armchairs.

This Left Bank Parisian apartment is graced with truly superb wooden boiseries included in the inventory of Historical Monuments. Dealing with such prestigious decorative elements certainly does not facilitate the decorator's role. National art treasures must, of course, be treated with due respect but should not be allowed to monopolize attention. What better way to pay homage to the Louis XIV carved wood paneling than to shift the interior towards the Napoleon III style? Alberto Pinto also lightens the rather grandiose décor through the use of warm colors on comfortable seating furniture and heavy draperies. In the foyer a bronze bust of Molière placed against wood paneling with stencilled gold leaf designs greets guests and prepares them for the theatrical stages that will follow. The slightly austere Regency boiserie with carved wood and gold panels in the sitting room is softened by scarlet velvet sofas and bergère armchairs. Although the bedroom walls are covered with Louis XVI paneling, the general tone is more 19th century. Some of the Empire furniture once belonged to Pauline Borghese.

The armoires, daybed and table once graced the private suite of the Princess Pauline, née Bonaparte. Pinto used the red and white striped wallpaper (pages 56–57) to connect the hall to the adjoining reception rooms, whereas areas used on a daily basis in the apartment are in peaceful tones of blue. The walls of the small sitting room, as well as those of the bedroom, are covered with pleated blue silk. The pale blue touches added to the Directoire wood paneling lighten the atmosphere of the dining room. The Russian furniture brings to mind the palatial luxury of Tsarkoï Selo and Pavlovsk. Engravings with stylish trompe l'œil frames line the walls of the hallways leading to the bedrooms, giving them an English flavor.

For an art collector

Rarely does a designer have the opportunity to design the same interior for different owners. Alberto Pinto first gave his personal twist to a Left Bank Paris apartment lined with historical, inventoried wood boiseries. Years later, an art collector called him for advice on how best to present his master paintings.

Whereas the first interior joyfully played with different decorative styles, introducing 19th-century Napoleon III elements in a characteristic Louis XIV style interior of the late 17th and early 18th centuries, Pinto's second vision of the space showed greater respect for historical coherence. Doors are adorned with painted designs that would not be inappropriate at the Château of Vaux-le-Vicomte. Casings are in faux marbre and walls are covered with Regency-style embossed velvet or silk brocade. In some rooms, wood paneling has been left unadorned.

An important collection of Impressionist works, as well as paintings by 20th-century masters such as Modigliani and Magritte, hang throughout the apartment. The study houses a series of marble busts that were already present in Pinto's first décor. It is interesting to note how well they suit both interiors, be it the later Louis XIV interpretation or the earlier 19th-century glittering opera-house version.

The antique wood paneling has been painted in the Louis XIV style. Alberto Pinto chose this stylistic period as the major theme of the interior, clearly announced in the painted design and bronze chandelier of the vestibule. This style statement, requiring equal doses of majesty and restraint, is also apparent in the study. The atmosphere in the sitting room is appropriate for contemplating the master works on display.

The generous scale and gentle simplicity of the dining room bring to mind provincial manor houses. The Beauvais tapestries, Venitian looking glass and antique marble urns balanced upon ionic marble columns are a feast for the eye.

The wood and gilt paneling in the main sitting room is a perfect backdrop for master paintings. There are no brash colors to interrupt the world of carved wood and gold; generous natural light enhances the quiet shades of blue. Discreet comfort is exemplified by Regency armchairs and large sofas covered in blue and reddish brown silks. Louis XIV-style chandeliers indicate the large scale of the reception rooms; in the sitting room, they have been hung higher than in the dining room, where more intimate lighting is required. Here, the form of the wood paneling accentuates the high ceilings. When adorned by a Beauvais tapestry, a Venitian mirror or marble medals, they go almost unnoticed.

The decoration of the bedroom has undergone a major mood change. The paneling has been painted in off-white thus enhancing the carved floral designs. The bed in the Louis XIV style (page 76–77) is surrounded by two studded velvet screens, creating a tranquil simplicity so conducive to restful slumber.

"Pied à terre" in New York

Guests entering this New York duplex are greeted by a Roman emperor in marble

By designing an interior in the grand English manor style, Pinto transformed this New York duplex to showcase a collection of European furniture. In the entranceway, a Roman emperor in marble stands proudly at the bottom of the staircase. Light floods through the tall windows in the main sitting room (pages 82–83). The alternating solid yellow and patterned velvet panels covering the walls only accentuate the brightness. Although different furniture styles have been combined, the superb quality of the pieces and an attentive eye to detail create a harmonious effect. Matching 18th-century French black lacquer commodes with bronze chinoiseries line one wall, while on the other side of the room, a collection of precious silver is displayed in a tall Boule bookcase, flanked by porphyre marble de Medici urns for symmetry. Crystal girandoles atop carved giltwood stands complete the grouping. Most of the seating furniture is Regency.

GREAT HOUSES OF ENGLAND & WALES
HUGH MONTGOMERY-MASSINGBERD CHRISTOPHER SIMON SYKES

PAVLOVSK The Collections

The main sitting room is an engaging combination of 18th–century furnishings. Groups of rare antique objects overrun the tables, like so many still life paintings.

The delightful clutter in the sitting room is actually a pretext to assemble still lifes of rare *objets d'art*: hardstone urns and porphyre vases here and there, rock crystal obelisks and silver boxes. A smaller sitting room doubles as a smoking room, its walls covered with Cordoba-style embossed leather. The typically English flavor is enhanced by a series of horse paintings (pages 90–91).

The fabric covering the walls of the English-style bedroom is caught behind crisscrossing ribbons. Billowing venetian blinds enhance the floral bed covers. Comfort is all-important in the private areas of the home, hence thick carpets, soft sofas, piles of cushions and pillows on the bed.

Quite often the point of departure for a bathroom design is a motif found on a engraved mirror, folding screen or carved wood panel. Here a Florentine marquetry pattern is repeated on closet doors and walls.

Following pages: The dining-room walls are covered with English chintz. The elegant curves of high-backed Chippendale chairs surround the table.

Town house in New York

In the foyer at the bottom of the stairway, a plaster statue of Hercules Linypus is proof of the owner's attachment to Neoclassical art. Playing the game of high theatrics which he knows so well, Pinto has brought together a French sofa by Cressent, Roman mosaics and an imposing movie spotlight.

In a seven-story mansion of particularly harmonious proportions, Alberto Pinto realized the difficult task of reconciling opposites for a New York art collector with decidedly eclectic tastes. The first impression of an apparently classical ambience is rapidly belied by a truly fanciful approach to presenting *objets d'art*. Conformity has been brushed aside in this world where Roman marbles, large film spotlights, Syrian mosaics and period French furniture are joyfully juxtaposed. A rare communion of tastes between owner and decorator has made *mélange* rule number one of the decorating game practiced here—and has turned the element of surprise into a minor art form. This typically American esthetic process has been slightly tempered by true European elegance.

Following page: In order to create a sense of intimacy in the spacious foyer, a Renaissance fireplace is flanked by consoles and English giltwood looking glasses.

The salon walls are covered with wide, solid-colored stripes struck with a Regency design. Treated as a *cabinet d'amateur*, the room is arranged in a provocative grouping of rare and extremely eclectic objects. The resulting atmosphere is nonetheless comfortable and intimate.

Two sculptures of sleeping children flank a serious family portrait above an unusual Boule armoire whose doors are decorated with portraits. In another corner, a black lacquer and gilt bronze desk (pages 102–103) stands between a pair of Dutch cabinets. The center of attention is the nearly three-meter-wide Thomire chandelier.

This imposing Italian bookcase is surmounted by a globe of the world and African masks. English furniture subtly mingles with French Regency armchairs.

The carefully studied lighting in the library makes it a true retreat for work and study. Sturdy wood-veneered shelves close off this area with bright blue brocade-covered walls. The owner's wide-ranging tastes discreetly pervade this apparently classical restrained space. Yet an African mask here, Chinese horses there, and an important Neoclassical painting above the fireplace (pages 104–105) are striking reminders that eclecticism is an art in itself.

Hung on a Regency design silk brocade, an 18th-century Venetian-looking glass presents engraved glass and giltwood decor in the pure Rococo style.

Reminiscent of an English men's club, the atmosphere in the dining room is deliberately masculine. The walls are covered in embossed leather and the comfortable chairs in leopard skins, like memories of safaris. A billiard table light fixture hangs over the table, while a large convex mirror above the sideboard reflects a wide-angle view of the room. Traditional accessories for London men's clubs—the painting of a fencer, the giant world globe—complete the pastiche.

The glasses are Russian engraved crystal.

Gentilhommière on the lake . . .

One of his most faithful clients asked Alberto Pinto to create an apartment in the French style for him in Geneva. Olive green silk brocade with a Regency design covers the foyer walls. A small round window adds intimacy to the space while enhancing its urbane character. Eighteenth-century bronzes are grouped on a Louis XVI console; across from it stand chairs in the style of Jacob.

Posed atop marble columns, Italian busts frame the entrance leading into sitting room (pages 116–117). There, Napoleon III capitonné sofas are surrounded by Louis XVI furniture (pages 118–119): commodes, consoles, a marquetry gueridon and those famous lyre-back chairs that Marie Antoinette so favored. The tender green wood paneling is set off by white sculpted motifs and moldings.

Louis XVI paneling and furniture reminiscent of Marie Antoinette serve as a backdrop to a collection of master paintings.

Throughout the sitting room, the shades atop the lamps are covered with almond green silk pleated shades. In this refined setting, a collection of modern masters grace the walls: a portait by Auguste Renoir, a bouquet by Marc Chagall…They add surprising twists to the dominant classical theme.

The dining-room walls (pages 122–123) are decorated with Neoclassical grotesques; a Russian cut-crystal chandelier hangs above a round table. A Boulle bronze and tortoiseshell marquetry complete the grouping.

Bedrooms are decorated with floral fabrics. Canopy beds offer the decorator an opportunity to create a quintessential feminine atmosphere.

Alberto Pinto chose floral motifs to enhance the comfort in the private areas of the apartment. The decorator quite naturally furnished the bedrooms with his signature canopy beds. They are an opportunity to juxtapose satin, silk and lace. Pleats, trims, braids are featured in this festival of passementerie. The beds are piled high with pillows and cushions. French furniture is also used throughout—for the Louis XVI sofa with its curved lines (opposite) and for the flowered-covered tub chairs.

A Summer House in Mexico

Inspired by Argentine haciendas and Texan farms, Alberto Pinto has fitted out an elegant summer mansion in Mexico, creating a tonic cross blend of Hispanic, Oriental and North American influences. Guests are welcomed under a peristyle leading to a column-lined patio in the Moresque style. Inside, Syrian mirrors with ornate mother-of-pearl inlays stand out against white walls and bare stone. The main sitting room is Near Eastern in flavor with oversized, pillow-covered divans lining the walls. Following the tradition of stately houses in southern Spain, interior doors and shutters are decorated with moucharabies. A seventeenth-century, haute-époque mood permeates the living spaces with dark wood antique furniture setting a rather severe tone. Hence, the dining room walls covered with traditional blue and white azulejos tiles bring to mind a refectory in a Portuguese convent. Elsewhere, a collection of Italian Majolica earthenware adds a touch of an ancient apothicary shop.

Simply hewn stone columns and and ornately carved wooden pillars dominate the Moresque entrance way.

Throughout the reception rooms wall
treatment is simple and rusticated to
make guests feel at home. Passementerie
details accent a refined choice of fabrics.

Alberto Pinto possesses a consummate talent for lighting. Here the ardor of the Mexican sun is transformed through decorative claustra and moucharabies shutters into delicate glowing lace.

Alberto Pinto calls into play years
of experience and unfailing intuition in
order to pass from the artist's rende-
rings of his studio to the real interior.

Following Pages:
The walls of this bedroom are covered
with stenciled botanical motifs of
medicinal plants and flowers.
The mahogany bed is nineteenth-
century Portuguese.

A blue house, the "Dune"

The delicate flesh tones of a French terracotta statue is a diversion in the blue and white house.

Alberto Pinto designed the interior of this seaside house in New York around the owner's all-consuming love for blue. Much more than a passing fancy inspired by the endless blue sky and water of the Hamptons, this monochromatic fetishism also pervades her other dwellings. The walls of the entranceway are sky blue, almost the color of periwinkle. The white lacquer paneling and staircase only intensify the effect. This direct, uncontrived contrast provides a clue to the elegant game of décor played throughout the house.

The dominant blue theme is announced in the entrance hall. Sky blue walls are decorated with blue and white porcelain.

The walls of the entranceway and the upstairs hall leading to the master bedroom suite are lined with an important collection of blue and white Chinese porcelain, relics from an 18th-century Dutch caravel, shipwrecked in the China Sea. The Dutch chandelier is, of course, in blue and white, as are the Regency armchairs, covered in blue and white velvet; bouquets echo the same color scheme. A 19th-century French terracotta statue of a Parisian grisette stands out because of its delicate pink tones.

This blue and white harmony is respected throughout the house – indeed, Pinto has no equal when it comes to sustaining such an emphatic design imperative. In the sitting room and dining room, lemon yellow English chairs and cushions are the surprising foil to the dominant colors. The 18th-century baroque painted screen and paneling create a contrasting effect in the dining room. The French pointillist paintings alone add a dissolute though discreet counter note of color.

A ranch in the desert

In the immense silence of the New Mexico desert, a ranch stands on a domain as vast as Manhattan Island. The scenery is the stuff films are made of and, quite naturally, *Dances with Wolves* was shot nearby. The architectural references are definitely South of the Border with an imposing pink and white hacienda dominating the exceptional site. The climate here has fascinating effects on the light: from one season to the next, snow and sun are constantly in concert or in conflict to produce very raw white lighting on the buildings.

A tireless builder called on the services of Alberto Pinto to furnish this country retreat. In much the same manner as a production decorator prepares for a period film, Alberto drew on childhood memories and his imagination to conjure up images of cowboys and Indians, masked avengers and gun-toting sheriffs.

In order to counterbalance the classical austerity, very comfortable South American sofas and armchairs upholstered with thick white fabric add a modern touch. Overleaf: English marble busts atop pedestals mark the beginning of a gallery of family ancestors.

With its Neo-Renaissance colonnettes and beige and gold paneling, the study takes us back to Elizabethan times—unless its stylistic references are actually those of the wooden cabins of 17th-century Portuguese caravels… The broken-angled coffered ceiling is an accomplished work of painted wood. The wooden bust is Spanish. The large English desk is flanked by antique world and celestial globes. The salon area is outfitted with an embossed deerskin sofa and two Italian armchairs. A leather chest placed between them serves as a coffee table. The cigar chest placed on it belonged to the Comte de Bestéguy.

With its ten-meter ceilings and a floor space twenty-five meters long and ten meters wide, the main salon that gives onto the patio provides a truly rare experience. In order to dramatize the already impressive volumes, an oversized Renaissance-inspired fireplace with two antique bronze caryatids is placed in the center. A suite of English paintings recounting a courtesan's life story line the stencilled walls. The velvet upholstered chairs are English.

In the sitting room comfortable conversation corners fan out
from the grand fireplace. Furniture is essentially English.
A suite of 17th-century paintings recount the activities of an
English courtesan under Charles II.

MISSION   Roger G Kennedy

The Gardens of SPAIN

TREASURES OF SPAIN

The fourth gallery off the patio serves as a summer dining room. As in the main salon, a fireplace is placed across from the bay window. The walls are adorned with a collection of large faïence plates decorated with the coats of arms of illustrious Florentine families. Chandeliers, floor lamps and dining-room furniture are in black wrought iron upholstered with wide-striped colored fabric.

The closed dining room is dominated by an important Dutch cabinet placed against a wall of 19th-century blue and brown azuleros tiles (pages 164–165). The Dutch table and the haute époque seats all contribute to the majestic atmosphere of this room, calling to mind a grand dining hall in a 17th-century château.

The Portuguese-inspired ceiling of the master bedroom is similar to that of the library. The broken-angled coffers are in painted wood. The thick wool rug is a clear indication of the simple comfort sought in this strict, masculine decor. Functionality was of prime importance in the stone bathroom (page 168). Nothing was added to distract from the breathtaking desert view through the immense window. The only concession is a carved wooden Austrian coatrack where carved teddy bears frolic. The shelves are English turned mahogany.

A studded natural leather
folding screen stands next to a
flannel–covered duchesse brisée.

The desert spreads out endlessly through the large picture window in this comfortable bathroom with its English furnishings and an amusing Austrian coatrack with teddy bears.

Summer residence in Marbella

Like an ever-evolving family house, this residence in Marbella has been regularly revamped and transformed by Alberto Pinto for a faithful client who has also entrusted him with the decoration of valued property around the world: houses and offices, as well as his yacht and private jet. Bathed by generous light year-round, the summer house is decorated in a voluntarily unaffected manner: white walls, wide bay windows, uncluttered space. The dining room is protected from the ardors of the Spanish sun by simple, unembellished shutters (pages 172–173). A tent draped from the ceiling onto the white walls enhances the impression of spaciousness. On the walls, blue and white Chinese porcelain has been symmetrically aligned on graphic consoles. The Dutch chandelier continues the color scheme with its Delft porcelain fittings; below it lies a 19th-century French petit point carpet. A round table is surrounded by bamboo cabriolet armchairs designed by the specialist Mac Guiere of San Francisco.

Vivid Chinese blues, striking consoles, and stunning pink orchids against sunny walls accentuate the carefree spirit of this summer residence in Marbella.

The small salon situated on the gallery near the patio is outfitted in natural shades of beige and white. Punched-tin lamps light raphia-covered tables.

The summer salon leads on to the patio. Two large punched-tin lamps are placed on woven raphia trompe l'œil tables by Bruno Roy. A collection of iridized hispano-moorish plates adorn the white walls. The majestic proportions of the grand salon are accentuated by the tent-draped ceiling so typical of grand Portuguese mansions. The dominating color scheme of beige and white for the furnishings and decoration was chosen by Alberto Pinto to confer a graceful airiness on the spacious room.

Surrounded by guest bedrooms, the small patio displays the traditional colors of Spain: red, yellow and white, the sand colors of bull rings and the ocres of sun-drenched soil. Even the large Chinese covered pots are saffron-colored. Illustrating different moods, each of the bedrooms reserves surprises for the guests. Pinto approached them as exercises in style. His theory about bedroom furnishings takes into consideration exactly how the rooms will be used. If they are to be used on a daily basis, a certain restraint should be exercised in outfitting them to avoid the boredom of overly anecdotal arrangements. However, rooms occupied by visiting friends can be opportunities for more whimsy. In one bedroom, Louisiana inspired the association of the colonnade bed, English engravings, mahogany and shocking pink. In another (pages 178–179), a modern Africa comes to mind. Here Pinto has brought together a woven straw commode, forties paintings, carved masks and a macassar floor lamp inspired by Brancusi's sculptures. A third bedroom (pages 180–181) has a definite lighthearted, Italian Dolce Vita, feminine influence with its mirror-covered furniture and Venetian armchair. A series of Italian faïence plates decorated with Turkish silhouettes adorns the pastel-colored walls.

Scarlett O'Hara would have felt at home in the colonial bedroom, as would have Karen Blixen in the African bedroom. The Italian bedroom with its carefree, Dolce Vita feeling awaits Anita Ekberg's visit.

A chalet in Courchevel

The wooden staircase with its distinctive turned balustrade is the soul of this mountain chalet.

When Alberto Pinto was commissioned to refurbish this old chalet in Courchevel, he demonstrated his architectural talents by completely restructuring the interior of the building.

A monumental staircase with a wooden railing became the heart of the dwelling. In order to take advantage of an exceptional view of the Alps, the sitting room is situated upstairs, while the downstairs bedrooms all open onto balconies.

All the reception rooms have traditional pine paneling, as does the vaulted ceiling. Moreover, the framework of the beams itself plays a significant role in the interior decoration. The paneling is in fact of the simplest kind; however, Pinto has added his personal touch by flanking the joists with a stencilled frieze. Door and window are framed by thick, elegantly curved moldings. A copper Dutch chandelier lights the sitting area.

The natural pine paneling and stencilled frieze infuse the atmosphere with elegant comfort. Overleaf: The furniture, like this copper chandelier, has haute époque lines.

The dining area is situated at the far end of the room around a long, sturdy wooden table. Large faïence plates hang on the walls. Coherence and tranquillity are achieved by maintaining the same color scheme for all the bedrooms: natural wood tones, beiges and off whites. In the master bedroom, light pine paneling is punctuated by marquetry designs similar to the cashmere patterns on the bedspread (page 188). Comfort is of prime importance here, as illustrated by the thick wool carpeting and the fur bed throw. Wooden floors, walls and furnishings adds cosiness to the bathrooms (page 189).

The exceptional view of the snow-covered Alps was reason enough for Pinto to devote the top floor to communal space, dividing the main living room into several sitting and dining areas.

After an invigorating day on the slopes, the warm, comfortable bedrooms on the lower level remind guests that they are here to relax. Pine, beige and off-white tones are omnipresent throughout the bedrooms and bathrooms.

A Left Bank dining room . . .
and pool

For friends in Paris, Alberto Pinto refurbished a delightfully French dining room. The walls are covered in simple wood paneling. Small carved-wood feathers placed on consoles flanking doors and wood panels around the walls add the whimsical Pinto touch. Spanish and Brazilian silver plates hang above. The haute époque chandelier spices up the multicultural design mixture, while a portrait by Victor Brauner focuses attention. The refined atmosphere situates the interior in the chic Seventh arrondissement, despite its surprising similarity to dining rooms in French country manors. Once again, Pinto masterfully juggles periods and styles.

This Left Bank dining room brings together 18th-century wood paneling and contemporary art objects.

A swimming pool has been added to the basement. Around it, azuleros tiles cover the walls in front of comfortable rattan chairs.

The architect Alain Raynaud chose Portuguese azuleros tiles to line the walls of the indoor Parisian swimming pool. In fresh blues and whites, the tiles reflect filtered light and echo the gentle gurgle of water in the wall fountain. Alberto Pinto displays on a painted wall a collection of Hispano-Moorish faience. Wide capitonné daybeds and rattan chaises longues offer comfort to swimmers.

A palace in Cairo

The challenge facing Alberto Pinto in this modern apartment building in Cairo was to join two separate spaces situated one above the other. Rather low ceilings were an additional hindrance. In such projects, the architect in Alberto takes over—his first instinct was to install a stairway in the center to connect the two floors. Light circulated from one space to the other, adding majesty to the interior, a majesty accentuated by the marble marquetry floor with a central rosace. Perfectly aligned windows on both levels disguise the lack of height.

Symmetrical sitting rooms flank the stairway. *Objets d'art* in ivory are grouped with other antiques on red shell and bronze tables (pages 200–201). The walls of a small sitting room are paneled in light-colored oak using a Versailles parquet design. Sitting furniture is covered with studded embroidered flannel. A collection of 19th-century bronze cups stands on a giltwood table (pages 204–205). Only the Islamic busts and the early-19th-century portrait evoke Egypt.

With Alberto Pinto's love of surprising cultural juxtapositions, it seemed completely natural to him to design a Moghul-inspired dining room within a Cairo palace. Travels to India and a stay in Jaipur brought him in direct contact with the comforts of Anglo-Indian luxury and inspired this spacious dining area, large enough for four or five big tables (pages 208–209). The large Moghul mural paintings set the tone of the room where columns and plinths are in repoussé silver. Chinese cloisonné elephants reinforce the exotic theme. Seats as well as the screen are covered with pearls and silver embroidered fabric. Pinto's India is actually a glorious jumble of cultures: English furniture, Chinese elephants, repoussé silver and a marble throne that once graced a garden in Parma.

A Russian flavor pervades the master bedroom. The walls are covered with embroidered brocade, using an antique design taken from a Lyonese pattern book.

Designing bathrooms provides an opportunity for Alberto Pinto to play with cultural references with surprising results— and why not hispanic ironwork in downtown Cairo? Given the setting, it would be natural to assume that Pinto's inspiration for the bathroom arose from Moorish mosques and hammams; however, Pinto takes great pleasure in crossing references, and in this case, a Louisiana plantation house served his fancy.

The panels of an Italian screen with mirror-covered medallions have been transformed into closet doors; their baroque design—straight from the set of a Visconti period film—was the point of departure for this space. Billowing fabric against beige and gilt paneling set the tone of opulent comfort.

Pinto's inspiration for both bathrooms was furnished by an antique object. Here he uses a mirror: the design of the 19th-century Florentine mirror in marquetry is repeated on wall paneling and cabinets. Hispanic wrought iron sets the tone in the other bathroom (page 211).

A large terrace on the top floor overlooking Cairo has been transformed into a dayroom with an adjoining bathroom for the master of the house. The tub, jacuzzi and daybed completely integrate the space, taking full advantage of the panorama of the teeming city below. Luxurious flooring largely contributes to the reigning opulence. Marble and hardstone marquetry rugs with seashell and coral designs decorate the marble floor.

An English mansion

Left and overleaf:
On the garden side, statues of
historical figures stand in the
circular Garden Hall: Henry VIII,
Anne Boleyn, Elizabeth I
and Sir Walter Raleigh.

Pages 220–221:
The Elizabethan dining room and
the Entrance Hall with a pair of
English cabinets decorated with
horse pictures.

Near Blenheim Palace in England, this historical residence at Glympton Park has been rebuilt and remodeled on several occasions since the 14th century, when the main block was built: in the 18th century, during the Victorian period and more recently by Philip Jebb. Alberto Pinto was asked to refurbish the interior and re-Georgianize the style. The reception rooms along the east and south side—the library, the sitting room, and the dining room—lead off from the circular Garden Hall and the main staircase. The walls of this imposing anteroom are painted with murals to look like tapestry. Four Victorian statues of Tudor and Elizabethan figures: Anne Boleyn, Henry VIII, Elizabeth I and Sir Walter Raleigh stand in the room. Leading off the garden hall, the dining room (pages 226–229) is in the Elizabethan manner: geometrical ribbed plaster ceiling, silver chandeliers, majestic oak table and wall hangings.

Rare English cabinets decorated with horse paintings (pages 220–221) flank the door leading from the entrance hall directly to staircase hall. Designed by Philip Jebb, the staircase (page 232) is impressive. Alberto Pinto's role was to enhance the general appearance of the hall which he achieved with ornamental trophies of arms, inspired by 17th-century royal armories. The carved pine paneling and fitted bookcases are quintessentially English. Leather chesterfields, horse paintings and book-lined shelves complete the picture.

*Philip Jebb designed the monumental
staircase, decorated by Alberto Pinto
with ornamental trophies of arms in
the 17th–century manner.*

*The master bedroom is
quintessential English comfort.
The canopy over the wide bed uses
a floral chintz; the same fabric also
covers the walls.
At Glympton Park Estate, Pinto
abandons his much-beloved
exoticism for once, creating a very
English atmosphere in England.*

The first-floor bedrooms are divided into suites with sitting rooms, bedrooms, bathrooms and dressing rooms. The walls of the master bedroom, as well as the bed canopy, are covered with a floral-patterned chintz. The carpet is decorated with a capitonné design in pure English style. Bedrooms designed by Pinto are always havens of comfort, and those at Glympton Park Estate are no exception. The theme for the bathroom (pages 238–239) comes from the highly ornate French mirror hanging over the sink (page 240), whose designs are repeated on the engraved mirrors of the closet doors.

*In the bathroom, mirrors reflect other
mirrors in endless repetition.
Round engraved mirrors, like
Bohemian crystal, grace the closet
doors. A delicate Baquès chandelier
hangs from the ceiling.*

On the Quai d'Orsay

The name of the game is Neoclassical monumentality, announced by ionic marble columns flanking the main sitting-room entrance. The wrought-iron Directoire doors are inspired by those of the Palais Royal in Paris.

When Alberto Pinto moved onto the quai d'Orsay overlooking the left bank of the Seine, he occupied the apartment that Roger Vivier, the celebrated shoe designer, had just left. Often photographed for interior design magazines, the shoe designer's interior was considered the epitome of style in the sixties and seventies. Vivier used his remarkable intuition to create surprising groupings. Abstract works by Soulages and César were juxtaposed with Louis XIV giltwood consoles, Italian glassware with Oriental sculpture. Alberto Pinto would impose his own ideas within his private world, a sort of design manifesto announcing the revival of elegant luxury on a grand style based on a delicate balance of nostalgia and grandeur.

In a more intimate style, the entrance to the private wing is guarded by bronze busts of Zeus and Hera set atop semi-circular German mahogany hat chests. The walls are lined with engraved views of French ports by Joseph Vernet, an important 18th-century French landscape artist.

In the main sitting room, Alberto Pinto wanted to achieve
the majestic eclecticism of mid-19th-century Russian palaces.
The choice of furnishings is pan-european. The chandelier is
Russian and the 19th-century clock is French. The table is
Austrian, and Pompeian gouaches evoke the Grand Tour
through classical Greece and Italy which rounded out the
education of young aristocrats.

The resolutely Neoclassical tone is enhanced by a twist of
monumentality. It is easy to forget that this riverside apartment
is located in the heart of Paris while the interiors are so
reminiscent of oversized halls in royal châteaux.

Pinto created two smaller areas with a more intimate atmosphere at either end of the main sitting room, on both sides of an Austrian table. To the right, highly ornate Empire sitting furniture is covered in stripes of panther and leopard skin fabric evoking 19th-century Central Europe. Two predominantly red English portraits—Pinto's signature color—hang on Venetian stucco walls.

To the left, an intimate corner with a large velvet capitonné sofa and pearl-embroidered cushions. On a table, a collection of iridized glassware from the Saint Louis crystalworks. Over the sofa hang two family portraits of unknown lineage.

The portrait of the woman is in the manner of Dubuffe. The terracotta group is by Carrier-Belleuse. The design of the doors is adapted from a French Empire model.

In the small yellow sitting room (pages 248–249), the walls are covered by a red-on-yellow-background toile de Jouy fabric by Burger, evoking the discovery of America. The motifs are framed by a bright green velvet bouclé ribbon. A similar crisscrossing of velvet ribbons on the walls creates a capitonné effect. The Boulle furniture, a Mazarin desk and an open-front bibliotheque are in red shell and copper marquetry. The family portrait from the school of Van Dyck adds panache.

The dining room is a precious case lined in emerald green velvet for the Russian dining table and chairs.

The emerald green velvet-covered walls provide a dramatic backdrop for an exceptional collection of blue and white Chinese porcelain presented on wooden consoles. The dramatic staging is completely voluntary. Pinto delights in organizing dinners, attending personally to the table decoration and menu in this dining room to create a feast for both the eye and palate. This dining room leads into the smoking room (pages 254–255). Covered with appliqué embroidered silk cushions, the sofa was adapted from the dress designer Paul Poiret's furniture. The walls are paneled with Cordovan leather on which are displayed 19th-century glazed platters inspired by Bernard Palissy.

The private wing in general and his bedroom in particular are treated like a very comfortable mid-19th-drawing room in a castle in Central Europe. Furnishings, however, come from England, Russia, France and the United States. Any flat surface is a pretext for an accumulation of *objets d'art* in silver, hardstone and carved wood.

*Under a 1903 portrait by
John Collier, a German
mahogany desk is overrun with
an accumulation of antiques,
drawings and flowers.*

Photography Credits

Georgio Baroni: 8, 10, 60, 61, 62-63, 64-65, 70-71, 72, 73, 74-75, 76-77, 78, 79, 80, 81, 82-83, 84-85, 88, 89, 90-91, 92, 93, 94-95, 96-97, 98-99, 100, 101, 102-103, 104-105, 106, 107, 108-109, 110, 111, 112, 113, 114, 115, 116-117, 118-119, 120, 121, 122-123, 124, 125,138, 139, 140-141, 142, 143, 144, 145, 146, 147,

Roland Beaufre: 16-17, 48-49, 51, 52-53, 54-55, 56-57, 58, 59, 126, 127, 128-129, 130, 131, 132-133, 134, 135-136, 137,

Jacques Dirand: 148, 149, 150-151, 152-153, 154, 155, 156-157, 158, 159, 160-161, 162, 163, 164-165, 166, 167, 168, 169, 198, 199, 200-201, 202-203, 204-205, 206, 207, 208-209, 210, 211, 212, 213, 214, 215, 216, 217,220-221, 231, 234-235, 237, 238-239,

Mark Fiennes: 216, 218-219, 228-229, 230, 231, 232, 233, 236, 240, 241,

Pascal Hinous: 182, 183, 184-185, 186, 187, 188, 189,

H. Millet: 50,

Jean-Baptiste Naudin: 2, 14, 15, 18, 19, 22-23, 25, 31, 32-33, 35, 36, 37, 38, 39, 40-41, 43, 44, 45, 46-47,

Studio Pinto: 26-27, 28-29, 66-67, 68-69, 86-87, 134, 135, 222-223, 224-225, 226-227.